M

NATURE WATCH
ZEBRAS

Written by
Lynn M. Stone

Lerner Publications Company • Minneapolis

To Mel Stone, for a lifetime of inspiration

Lerner Publications Company
A division of Lerner Publishing Group, Inc.
241 First Avenue North
Minneapolis, MN 55401

Website address: www.lernerbooks.com

Library of Congress Cataloging-in-Publication Data

Stone, Lynn M.
  Zebras / by Lynn M. Stone.
    p.   cm. — (Nature watch)
  Includes index.
  ISBN 978–0–8225–7511–5 (lib. bdg. : alk. paper)
  1. Zebras—Juvenile literature. I. Title.
QL737.U62S763 2009
599.665'7—dc22   2007023948

Manufactured in the United States of America
1 2 3 4 5 6 – DP – 14 13 12 11 10 09

CONTENTS

A family group of Grevy's zebras eats grass on the Kenyan countryside.

ZEBRAS

NEARLY ALL THE ANIMALS THAT SHARE THE YELLOW AND green plains of Africa are the muted colors of dust and soil. **Predators'** fur is colored in earth tones that disguise them as they hunt. Most of the grazing animals—the **prey** animals like impalas, wildebeests, topis, and gazelles—also blend easily into the waving **savanna** grasses. Their color helps them to escape their pursuers.

Compared to their neighbors, zebras seem out of place. Herds of zebras thunder across the plains in a dizzying array of black-and-white stripes. They almost seem to be the work of an artist who has painted dazzling black stripes on white ponies.

Scientists have offered many explanations of why a zebra has stripes. One is that stripes blend in nicely with tall, waving grasses. The stripes offer the zebra **camouflage**. Lions, the zebra's main predators, are thought to be color blind. So the striped pattern helps zebras more than a color scheme would. Perhaps a herd of striped animals confuses lions. A lion may have difficulty singling out one animal from the herd's bundle of stripes, especially if the herd is moving.

Plains zebras have wide stripes. Their light stripes are creamy white.

ZEBRAS AND HORSES

Zebras are as wild as the winds that rush across Africa's plains. Still, zebras share bloodlines with one of the world's beloved domesticated animals, the horse. In body structure and body chemistry, a zebra is basically a small horse with stripes.

Zebras are grazing animals, like their domesticated cousins. And like horses, zebras can be long lived. A study showed

Some plains zebras have shadow stripes. These grayish stripes break up large white stripes.

While stripes may make it difficult for predators to pick out zebras, stripes probably make it easier for zebras to pick out other zebras. Like fingerprints, a zebra's stripe pattern is one of a kind, specific to that individual zebra. Some **zoologists** believe the unique stripe patterns help zebra **foals** and their mothers find each other more easily.

Grevy's zebras have narrow stripes. Their light stripes are bright white.

that in one wild population of zebras, the average age was 9. But captive zebras have lived more than 30 years.

Zebras and horses belong to the same **genus**, *Equus. Genus* is a scientific term for a group of different but closely related creatures. Members of the genus *Equus* are called **equids**.

The genus *Equus* is part of a larger group, the order Perissodactyla. This order includes all hoofed mammals—the equids, plus tapirs and rhinoceroses. All perissodactyls have a similar bone structure in their feet. These animals are adapted to running.

Many people have attempted to tame zebras. Zebras have appeared in circuses. They have been trained to pull wagons. Occasionally they have been trained to carry riders on their backs. They have been bred with horses, ponies, and donkeys to create **hybrid** equids. But on the whole, zebras have been failures as working animals.

Left: This hybrid is a cross between a zebra and a horse. It is sometimes called a zorse. *Below:* A herd of plains zebras visits a water hole. Predators may find it hard to single out one zebra from another in the herd.

ZEBRAS OF
MANY STRIPES

MOST ZOOLOGISTS AGREE THAT THE GENUS *EQUUS* includes seven **species**. They are the domestic horse, the African wild ass (including donkeys and burros), the Asian wild ass (including the kulan and the onager), the kiang, the plains zebra, the mountain zebra, and Grevy's zebra. A fourth species of zebra, the quagga, died out in the wild in the late 1870s. It became extinct when the last captive quagga died in Amsterdam, the Netherlands, in 1883.

The plains zebra is the most common of the three living species of zebra. It is the only wild equid whose future seems fairly secure. Tens of thousands of plains zebras still live on the African plains. They have about 26 stripes on each side of their body. The stripes are wider than those of other zebra species. Most plains zebras weigh 640 to 750 pounds (290–340 kg). They make a barking sound to communicate with one another.

The mountain zebra lives in Namibia and South Africa. It is about the same size as the plains zebra. Its population had decreased for many years, but it has begun to grow slowly. Mountain zebras have about 55 stripes on each side. They neigh like horses.

The increasingly rare Grevy's zebra is found mainly in northern Kenya. Only a few thousand are left. Grevy's zebra is the largest of all the living equids. It weighs up to 1,000 pounds (450 kg). It has narrower stripes than other zebras—about 80 stripes on each side. It also lives in more **arid** country than other zebras. Grevy's zebras make a braying sound similar to a donkey's.

SUBSPECIES

Among the plains and mountain zebra populations are groups that scientists call **subspecies**. Within each zebra species, such as the mountain zebra, members have far more similarities than differences. But some minor differences occur over the animals' geographic range. The differences are typically in size, striping, or voice. If zoologists find enough minor differences, they may decide that a certain geographic population differs enough from another to be called a subspecies.

For example, zoologists recognize two mountain zebra subspecies. They are the Cape mountain zebra and the Hartmann's mountain zebra. The two mountain zebra subspecies live in somewhat different environments. The Cape mountain zebra is shorter and stockier than the Hartmann's mountain zebra. The Cape mountain zebra is the smallest of all the zebras. **Mares**, or females, weigh a little more than 500 pounds (230 kg). It has longer ears and a larger dewlap than a Hartmann's mountain zebra. The dewlap is a loose flap of skin under the animal's throat.

This quagga lived in the London Zoo. This photo was taken in 1870.

Generally, plains zebras in southern Africa have fewer stripes and are lighter in color than plains zebras in northern Africa. The quagga, which lived in southern Africa, had dark brown stripes only on its head, neck, and forequarters. A growing number of zoologists think that the quagga may have been a kind of plains zebra. DNA analysis supports this idea.

Zoologists usually divide plains zebras into five subspecies. They are the Chapman's, Crawshay's, Damara, Grant's, and Upper Zambezi plains zebras. The most obvious differences among the plains subspecies are the animals' stripes and size. On average, Damara plains zebras, the southernmost subspecies, have fewer stripes than do Grant's plains zebras, the northernmost subspecies. Damara zebras are about one-third larger than Grant's zebras. The plains zebra subspecies also show small differences in their teeth and skull structure.

"Wild" horses such as the mustangs of the western United States are not truly wild. They are feral horses—untamed animals descended from domestic horses that escaped into the wild.

Above: Crawshay's plains zebras keep watch in South Luangwa National Park in Zambia.
Inset: The Cape mountain zebra has long ears and reddish brown stripes on its nose. It also has a dewlap, a flap of skin on its neck.

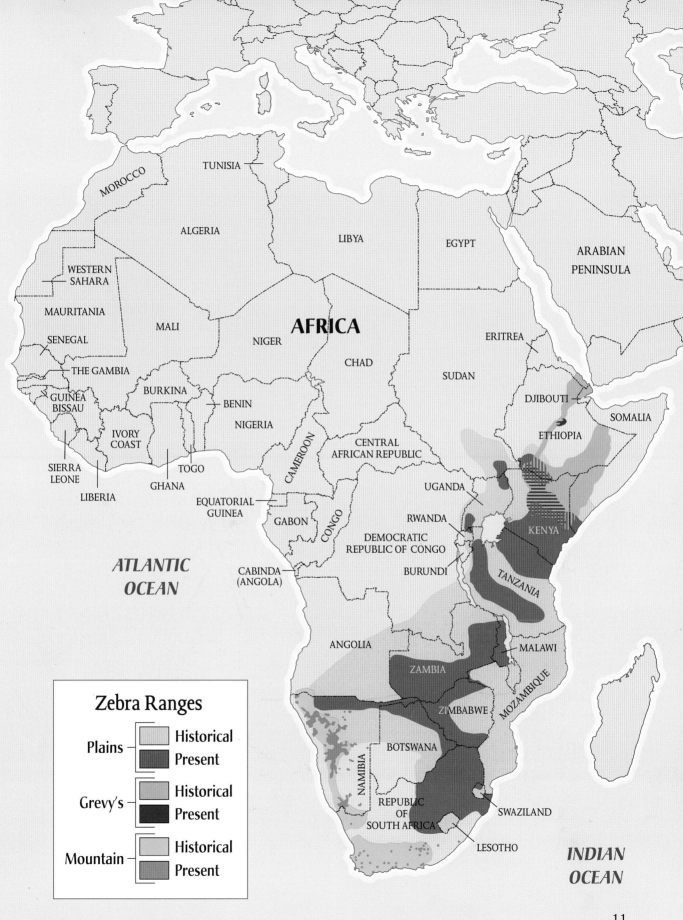

Zebra Ranges

Plains
- Historical
- Present

Grevy's
- Historical
- Present

Mountain
- Historical
- Present

MOROCCO
TUNISIA
ALGERIA
LIBYA
EGYPT
ARABIAN
PENINSULA
WESTERN
SAHARA
MAURITANIA
MALI
AFRICA
NIGER
CHAD
ERITREA
SUDAN
DJIBOUTI
SOMALIA
SENEGAL
THE GAMBIA
BURKINA
BENIN
NIGERIA
ETHIOPIA
GUINEA
BISSAU
IVORY
COAST
TOGO
CENTRAL
AFRICAN REPUBLIC
UGANDA
SIERRA
LEONE
GHANA
CAMEROON
KENYA
LIBERIA
EQUATORIAL
GUINEA
GABON
CONGO
RWANDA
DEMOCRATIC
REPUBLIC OF CONGO
BURUNDI
TANZANIA
ATLANTIC
OCEAN
CABINDA
(ANGOLA)
ANGOLA
MALAWI
ZAMBIA
MOZAMBIQUE
ZIMBABWE
NAMIBIA
BOTSWANA
REPUBLIC
OF
SOUTH AFRICA
SWAZILAND
LESOTHO
INDIAN
OCEAN

11

ZEBRA COUNTRY

PLAINS ZEBRAS, THE MOST WIDESPREAD SPECIES, OCCUR from southern Ethiopia to central Angola and eastern South Africa. Nearly 7 of every 10 plains zebras live in just two countries: Kenya and Tanzania. Grevy's zebras are limited to southern and eastern Ethiopia and northern Kenya, with perhaps a tiny population in Sudan. Mountain zebras live in Namibia and South Africa.

For the most part, each zebra species or subspecies lives apart from others. Grevy's and plains zebras, however, overlap on the floodplain of the Ewaso Nyiro River in northern Kenya. The two species **graze** together, but apparently they have not **interbred**.

Within the vast African landscape, each zebra population has a preferred living area called its **habitat**. The plains zebra has adapted to a greater variety of habitats than other zebras. Plains zebras prefer open country—grasslands and the broad African savannas of grass and scattered trees. But they are also found in lightly wooded areas and even on towering mountain slopes more than 13,000 feet (4,000 m) high. They avoid deserts, wetlands, and thick forests.

Grevy's zebras live on grasslands and shrublands in arid and semiarid country. Although they tolerate dry country, they need a permanent source of freshwater. They cannot go more than five days without water.

Mountain zebras do not frequent the high mountain altitudes that plains zebras sometimes do. But they do live up to 6,500 feet (2,000 m) above sea level. That is about the same altitude as the highest peaks of the Appalachian Mountains in the eastern United States. Mountain zebras live on the slopes of mountains in southern Africa.

Right: **Plains zebras graze alongside a giraffe in eastern Africa.**
Below: **Plains zebras race across the Okavango Delta in Botswana.**

Lions, elephants, and leopards live in both Africa and Asia. Zebras, however, are strictly African animals.

Many zebra populations do not spend the entire year in one area. With seasonal changes in temperature and rainfall, zebras may move from higher elevations to lower ones. For example, mountain zebras live in lush, high-altitude pastures during the summer. They leave for lower, warmer pastures when winter cold sweeps onto the mountain heights. On the plains, some Grevy's zebras and plains zebras make regular **migrations**, following the rains to greener pastures.

A lone wildebeest joins a herd of plains zebras in their migration across the Makgadikgadi Pans National Park in Botswana.

ZEBRAS ON THE MARCH

THE LARGEST ZEBRA MIGRATION TAKES PLACE ON THE Serengeti Plain of Tanzania and Kenya. It is one of the great wildlife spectacles on the planet. It involves tens of thousands of plains zebras and perhaps one million wildebeests and Thomson's gazelles. Wildebeests and Thomson's gazelles are two antelope species that are common in eastern Africa.

The animals are driven on by nature's promise of greener grass wherever the rains fall. They follow storm clouds in a counterclockwise loop from Tanzania north into Kenya and back. For migratory wildebeests and zebras, travel is a way of life. The animals move throughout much of the year. Wherever the herds gather, the land seems alive with their snorts, squeals, grunts, and bellows.

Plains zebras keep an eye on a hunting cheetah on the Masai Mara National Reserve in Kenya.

Lions are attracted to the migration because it offers them plenty of animals to hunt. After the animals trudge on, the plains where they had been lie empty except for little piles of white bones. These lion leftovers are evidence of the hazards of migration.

Migration is a dangerous business for grazing animals. River crossings are special challenges. One gray September day in Kenya, a mixed herd of several hundred migrating plains zebras and wildebeests pauses near the Mara River, the latest peril in their journey. The animals mill about on a grassy flatland within a few strides of shore. Some graze. Others stand quietly, switching their tails to ward off flies. The herd is paralyzed by instinctive caution.

Antelopes are swift, graceful grazing animals. All antelopes have horns, although in some species, horns are found only on the males. Africa is home to a wide variety of antelopes, including wildebeests, Thomson's gazelles, impalas, and springboks. They range in size from the royal antelope, which is 10 inches (25 cm) tall at the shoulder, to the giant eland, which is 70 inches (180 cm) tall.

The caution is well placed. Here at a bend, the rushing river is no more than 50 yards (46 m) across, but it is swollen and muddied by rain. Bushes along the near shore are ideal hideaways for lions. And the elder animals among the waiting herd must certainly have learned from experience that crocodiles live in rivers. Crocodile jaws, no less surely than a lion's, can end their lives. The zebra's wide-vision eyes, keen ears, and fine sense of smell are helpful in identifying predators in open country. But they are useless in spotting crocodiles. Crocs cruise underwater or wait at the surface, looking like harmless floating logs.

The likely place for the herds to begin a crossing is not steep, but neither is it wide. A trail runs diagonally down from the plain to the river's edge. When the animals come to the river, they must file down the narrow trail no more than two abreast.

A zebra spots a crocodile and leaps back toward the bank of the Mara River while the rest of the herd retreats to safety.

About 1 mile (1.6 km) downstream from the crossing site is an island of branches at a curve in the Mara. Trees uprooted by the rain-swollen river have tangled together. Caught on the branches are the bodies of zebras and wildebeests, drowned animals that could not beat the current. The jumble of sticks and carcasses is a feast for squabbling vultures. The birds teeter on overhead limbs and then flap down to gorge themselves.

The Mara River winds through Kenya and Tanzania. The Masai Mara National Reserve takes part of its name from the river.

Vultures and a marabou stork feast on the bodies of animals drowned during the Mara crossing.

On the far side of the river, a low, muddy bank offers an easy exit. Above and beyond it lies new pasture on high ground. But to reach this exit bank, the animals must swim a short distance upstream, against the river's flow. An animal that is not strong enough to defeat the current must either come ashore under an impossibly steep bank directly across the river or be swept downstream. For the nervous zebras and wildebeests, neither option must seem appealing.

Plains zebras join a herd of wildebeests at the Mara River crossing.

Meanwhile, upstream at the crossing, the herd is becoming increasingly restless. Their migration is necessary. The Mara River has delayed the animals, but it will not stop them. The herds will continue to follow the seasonal rains and graze on the lush grass ahead, even if they must plunge into the Mara to do so. The question is not *whether* the herds will wade into the brown river. The question is *when*.

The restlessness grows. A few zebras shuffle away from the mass and move closer to the riverbank. One trots down the path to the river's edge. Two more follow abruptly. No lions spring from beneath the bushes. The zebras wade into the river and swim upstream. Only the animals' heads stay above the water. Their legs stride powerfully underwater, taking these zebras to the easy exit on the far shore.

Reassured, more zebras and a pair of wildebeests trot down the shoreline path. Moments later, most of the herd edges forward onto the low bluff over the Mara. Soon a lengthening thread of galloping animals fills the trail leading to the river. Some animals plunge into the river easily. Others, unsure, snort and trot nervously in the shallows. But eventually

Right: A crocodile attacks a zebra foal in the Mara River. Young zebras are particularly vulnerable during the crossing.

A zebra struggles against the current in a difficult river crossing.

Plains zebras leap to safety after crossing the Mara River.

they too are forced into the river by the growing crowd of animals behind them.

The zebras and wildebeests, dozens of them now, splash into the Mara. Animals are everywhere in the river and on both shores. A few animals struggle with the current. One wildebeest, its horned head just above the surface, slips downstream, where it disappears around a bend. It is not a good direction to go. Several wildebeests wade ashore below the high, muddy bank. This is the bank they cannot climb. They will have to reenter the river and swim upstream. They are bedraggled and dripping and as dark as the mud in which they stand. They show little interest in another swim. But in minutes, giving in to their desperate need to continue the migration, they will wade back into the current. There is no other way to rejoin the herd.

Twenty minutes pass. The crossing ends as suddenly as it began. The grassy plain on the near side of the river is empty and quiet. All the animals have taken the Mara plunge. On this day, nearly all of them have survived.

LIFE IN
ZEBRA SOCIETY

LIKE HORSES, ZEBRAS ARE SOCIAL ANIMALS—THEY LIKE ONE another's company. They tend to live in small groups called **bands.** The bands form the social structure of a zebra's life. Sometimes several bands meet up during migration or at a particularly good grazing area. The bands come together to form large, loose herds. Zebra **stallions** from different bands greet one another with snorts, head bows, and rubbing of heads and shoulders.

Among plains zebras and mountain zebras, bands are either family groups or groups of stallions. The family bands are called **harems.** They consist of a **dominant** stallion, 1 to 6 adult mares, and their offspring. Most harems have 4 to 8 individuals, but they may have as many as 15. Stallion bands are called **bachelor bands**. They average 2 or 3 stallions, but they may have up to 16 members.

Maintaining a harem is every stallion's goal. This drive is as powerful as the urge to eat and drink. An adult stallion without a harem is always on the lookout to gather mares from other harems and start his own. But to do so, he must overcome the mares' current stallion. Kick-and-bite fights are common between stallions that are trying to win mares. A stallion can keep his harem as long as he remains strong enough to defend it against other stallions. Some stallions keep their harems for as long as 15 years.

Mares often remain in the same harem for many years. They may stay even after they are too old to bear foals. A mare may leave her harem if the stallion is defeated by a younger, stronger stallion. Individual mares may also be "stolen" by other stallions.

Above: Zebras kick and bite in a struggle for dominance. *Left:* This family band of Crawshay's zebras lives in South Luangwa National Park in Zambia.

Above: A Grevy's zebra foal frolics alongside its mother.
Right: A lone Grevy's zebra stallion blends into the brown grasslands.

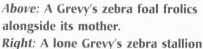

NOT-SO-SOCIAL ZEBRAS

Grevy's zebras are not as social as plains and mountain zebras. The only strong relationships among Grevy's zebras are between mares and their young offspring. The mares and foals may be part of loose groups that also include young males and females without offspring. Zebras come and go from these groups, which often number between 20 and 50 animals.

Many Grevy's stallions spend much of the year by themselves. They live on a large plot of land they defend as a territory. A stallion's territory may be larger than 4 square miles (10 sq. km). A stallion marks the boundaries of his territory with urine and droppings. These scent posts tell other stallions to stay away.

A Grevy's stallion may control his territory for several years and leave it only to find water or join a migration. Ideal territories have plenty of ground plants and standing water. This makes them attractive to mares. When mares enter the stallion's territory, he attempts to herd them away from any other stallions that are nearby. The territorial stallion will tolerate young stallions on his territory, but not mature stallions. The territorial stallion will charge, bray at, and bite and kick other stallions.

Harem life has certain advantages. Multiple animals mean more eyes watching for predators. A stallion will fight to protect the members of his harem. A harem's stallion and mares also do not have to search for mates during the breeding season.

Each zebra in a group has a **rank**. Rank is a zebra's social position compared to other zebras. Higher-ranking zebras are dominant over lower-ranking zebras. High-ranking stallions are those who defeat other stallions in fights. Mares show dominance by kicking and biting other mares.

ZEBRA NEIGHBORHOODS

Zebras that do not migrate occupy a **home range** throughout the year. The home range is a broad grazing area. Each band or harem has its own home range, but ranges overlap. Unlike territories, which are property to be defended, home ranges are shared neighborhoods.

Cape mountain zebras do not migrate and seldom gather in large herds. This pair belongs to a small family group living in Mountain Zebra National Park in South Africa.

Home ranges vary in size from less than 2 square miles (less than 5 sq. km) to more than 200 square miles (more than 500 sq. km). Home ranges tend to be larger during the drier months when food is scarce, forcing the zebras to travel a greater distance.

Zebras feed mostly during daylight, grazing up to half of the time that they are awake. When they are not eating, zebras rest, rub against trees and rocks, and roll on the ground. Rubbing and rolling help a zebra rid itself of pesky insects, loose hair, and dead skin. Like a massage, rolling probably just feels good too.

Zebras sleep during the night. Like horses, zebras can sleep lying down or on their feet.

Above: A plains zebra takes a dust bath in the Masai Mara in Kenya.
Left: Two plains zebras groom each other.

Zebras use their strong teeth and flexible lips to graze on short grasses and tree leaves.

Zebras also groom one another. They nibble on one another's necks, manes, and backs. Grooming may last a few minutes or for half an hour. Zebras don't really need their manes combed. Grooming is largely a way for zebras to form close social bonds within harems or bands. Plains zebras groom one another more than other zebra species.

A pair of Chapman's plains zebras nibbles on new grass growing after a rainstorm.

EATING AND BEING EATEN

Among grazing animals, zebras are somewhat unusual. They are the only African plains grazers with both upper and lower **incisor** teeth. Antelopes and other grazers have a hard gum pad instead of upper incisors. They press their lower incisors against the pad to tear off grass or leaves. Two sets of incisors allow zebras to bite off tough parts of grass plants. When plants are scarce on the ground, zebras eat the leaves of trees.

Zebras can eat many different kinds of plants. That means they can live in a wider variety of habitats than most large mammals of the African plains. Plains zebras can thrive on some poor-quality grasslands. Migratory zebras can find food wherever they travel.

A young male lion chases a mixed herd of plains zebras, springboks, and wildebeests in Etosha National Park, Namibia.

The food zebras eat is not very **nutritious**. They have to eat a lot to get enough of the substances their bodies need. A zebra's digestive system processes food quickly, so the animal can eat more each day.

The zebras in a harem or band don't all graze at the same time. One or more zebras are always on guard duty, looking for predators such as lions. Zebras watch for sudden movements and for the outlines of predators lurking in the grass.

When a predator approaches, speed is a zebra's best defense. When fleeing for its life, a zebra can run 35 to 40 miles per hour (56–64 km/hour). It can't run far at that speed, but it doesn't have to. If a lion does not quickly succeed in catching a zebra, it will give up on the chase and wait for an easier meal. Catching up with a zebra doesn't guarantee a lion a meal, either. An adult zebra's powerful kicks can seriously injure a predator.

ZEBRAS
BORN AND RAISED

ONE OF THE MOST IMPORTANT BONDS IN ZEBRA SOCIETY is between stallions and mares. In the harems of mountain and plains zebras, mares may stay with a single stallion for years. Harem bosses come and go, however. Mares led by one stallion for years may eventually be taken by another stallion. Among Grevy's zebras, there are no lasting bonds between stallions and mares.

When a mare's body is almost ready to conceive a foal, she goes into a period of **estrus**. This period lasts roughly two weeks to a month. During estrus, the mare's body gives off a scent that stallions recognize. The scent signals the mare's readiness to mate.

Dominant mountain and plains zebra stallions with harems may have their older mares to themselves. But both harem and bachelor stallions may pursue a young mare in her first estrus. The result is often loud,

Above: **A pregnant zebra *(left)* in Etosha National Park, Namibia**
Right: **A plains zebra gives birth in Kenya. The foal is covered in a thin sac of skin, which the mother licks off soon after the birth.**

squealing fights between stallions. Fights usually end without serious damage to either stallion. The dominant stallion chases away his challenger.

Dominant stallions mate with the mares. Once pregnant, mountain zebra and plains zebra mares carry their foals for about a year. Grevy's mares carry their babies for approximately 13.5 months. Each mare usually bears a single foal, not twins or triplets.

Zebras are born throughout the year. The peak birthing times for Grevy's zebras are August through September and November through December. Peak time is December through February for Cape mountain zebras and November through April for

Hartmann's mountain zebras. Plains zebras in East Africa generally give birth during the wet season, October through March. Elsewhere, the peak birthing season varies. After foaling, a zebra mare may not give birth again for up to 3 years.

The largest zebra foals are Grevy's. They average about 85 pounds (39 kg). Plains zebra foals weigh about 70 pounds (32 kg), and mountain zebra foals weigh about 55 pounds (25 kg).

A baby zebra stands almost immediately after its birth. It instinctively begins to nurse on its mother's milk. It can run within an hour or two. Then it can keep up with a moving herd and make itself a more difficult target for predators.

A newborn plains zebra foal stands up for the first time as its mother watches for danger.

Grevy's foals are quite unusual. They are born brown and black, lacking the adult pattern of black-and-white stripes. Their manes are also unusual. All zebras have a bristly mane along their necks. But the mane of a newborn Grevy's zebra runs along its back from neck to tail!

31

Zebra foals begin to nibble grass at the age of about a week. They eat more grass as they grow older and larger, but they also continue to nurse. When they are about 10 months old, their mothers **wean** them by refusing to let them nurse.

Weaned youngsters are nearly full grown, and they are fairly independent. But they still travel closely with their mothers. They may stay with mom for up to 2 more years. Then they leave their birth harems. They find other bands to join.

Right: **This plains zebra foal was born in Zambia.**
Below: **Mountain zebra foals nurse.**

Young male plains zebras start their own family groups when they are strong enough to challenge older stallions for mares. This family group is traveling through a Kenyan nature reserve.

Young zebras are able to start their own families at 3 or 4 years of age. Stallions, however, are usually at least 4 years old before they can challenge older males for mares. Grevy's males are usually 6. Studies have shown that some mountain zebra mares are 6 years old before they give birth to their first foal.

ZEBRAS IN THE GRASSLAND COMMUNITY

THE AFRICAN GRASSLAND IS A DYNAMIC COMMUNITY OF plants and animals. A healthy grassland has a wonderful alphabet stew of animals: antelopes, buffaloes, cobras and cranes, egrets and elephants, giraffes, impalas, leopards and lions, oryxes, ostriches and oxpeckers, topis and Thomson's gazelles, warthogs and wildebeests, and zebras. All these animals help to keep the grasslands healthy.

Plains zebras are especially important in the health of their communities because they are far more numerous than Grevy's or mountain zebras. The grazing habits of plains zebras help other grass eaters. Plains zebras often move into a new grazing area before other animals do. They eat the tougher parts of grass plants. That leaves the tender parts for animals such as wildebeests and Thomson's gazelles, which can't eat the tough food zebras can.

Zebras also help distribute plant seeds. A zebra does not digest everything it eats. Many seeds, for instance, pass through its digestive system. They are returned to the plains in the zebra's manure. Some of those seeds may eventually be eaten by animals such as birds and mice, but others sprout into new plants.

Many animals depend on acacia trees on the Masai Mara *(left)* for food. Zebras eat seed pods that fall from the trees. Some seeds are dropped in zebra manure and sprout into new trees.

Black rhinos and plains zebras graze on many of the same kinds of plants.

Above: **Zebra mares must protect their foals from predators. This mare keeps herself between her foal and a pursuing cheetah.**
Right: **This leopard has killed a zebra foal. Leopards sometimes eat their prey in trees to keep other predators from stealing it.**

Zebras help plants in other ways too. When zebras walk or run, their hooves help to loosen the soil. That helps plants' roots grow down into the ground. Zebras' droppings return **nutrients** to the soil. Nutrients help plants grow.

Zebras and other **herbivores** (plant eaters) also provide energy for **carnivores** (meat eaters). Large herbivores are prey for large carnivores, including lions, spotted hyenas, wild dogs, leopards, and crocodiles. Cheetahs are not a threat to healthy, adult zebras, but they can kill foals. After the predators have eaten their fill, zebra carcasses feed **scavenging** vultures, hyenas, and marabou storks.

Although predators kill individual zebras, they are not a threat to the wild zebra population. The zebras' future depends on the actions of people, not predators.

Above: Spotted hyenas eat a young zebra. Behind them, vultures wait for their turn. *Right:* After vultures and other scavengers finish eating, insects feed on the remains of the zebra. Within a few days, only the skeleton remains.

SAVING
ZEBRAS

PERHAPS MORE THAN 1 MILLION WILD ZEBRAS LIVE IN
Africa today. That seems like a large number of zebras. But it is far fewer
than in the recent past. In the late 1970s, about 15,000 Grevy's zebras
lived in Africa. Now there may be 5,000. As recently as 1985, plains
zebras lived in nearly all the countries of southern, eastern, and south-
western Africa. That is no longer the case.

Zebras live in some remote places, but they also live in rural areas.
There they share land and water with livestock and people. As the
human population grows, the African wilderness shrinks. More and
more open wildlands become farmland. Irrigation systems move water
from natural sources to farms. Livestock graze where once only wild
animals lived. Increasingly, zebras have to compete with cattle for grass
and water. Some farmers welcome wildlife on their lands, but others

erect fences around their land and water, keeping wildlife away.

Africa's population growth and expansion into the countryside is a growing problem for wildlife. But a bigger concern is the lack of political stability in many African nations. In recent years, power struggles and civil wars have raged in Angola, Democratic Republic of the Congo, Uganda, Sudan, Somalia, Rwanda, and other countries. Warfare has killed huge numbers of people and wildlife. It has also frightened away tourists, whose dollars helped to establish and maintain Africa's national parks and game reserves. Even countries that have escaped warfare have struggled with poverty and changes in governments and lifestyles. Many African nations have lacked the will, manpower, and money to protect wildlife. Human suffering and survival have been more important issues.

Yet some African nations with zebras, such as South Africa, Malawi, Zimbabwe, Namibia, Botswana, Tanzania, and Kenya, have managed to protect at least some of their wildlands and wildlife.

Above: **Plains zebras graze in Nairobi National Park, outside of Nairobi, Kenya. Because the park is so close to the city, urban sprawl and pollution have a big impact on wildlife in the park.**
Opposite: **A park ranger in Nairobi National Park, Kenya, cares for orphaned elephants and zebras.**

For example, wildlife is protected in about one-fourth of the entire country of Tanzania. Tanzania's Serengeti National Park is home to the world's single largest zebra population—more than 150,000 plains zebras. The hunting of zebras for meat still threatens many herds outside of the protected areas, however. Kenya has a world-famous chain of national parks, but only about 10 percent of its zebras live in them.

Left: A park ranger and two Masai warriors *(in red)* lead tourists on a game walk in Masai Mara National Reserve. *Below:* Zebras graze in Serengeti National Park, Tanzania.

Above: Curious dogs watch as a zebra nibbles grass at the edge of a farm. Zebras sometimes anger farmers by crossing fences and grazing on crops.
Left: A zebra greets tourists at an African national park.

No animal can survive without a place to call home. Providing more lands where wildlife is protected, in Kenya and elsewhere in Africa, would certainly help zebras. But in the years ahead, zebras will need more than a home. They will need African governments and African people who are committed to protecting their natural heritage. African governments will also need help from other countries in the form of money and tourism.

People can destroy zebras. Dutch and British settlers in South Africa proved that more than a century ago. They wiped out the Burchell's subspecies of plains zebras and the quagga. But people also can save zebras. Modern-day South Africans are showing this in their work with Cape mountain zebras. In 1937, researchers counted just 45 Cape mountain zebras. A few more probably lived in remote mountains. Since then, the population has expanded to about 1,300, and

In Namibia, the population of Hartmann's mountain zebras seems to be gradually decreasing. On the other hand, the **endangered** Cape mountain zebra population has steadily grown in South Africa, where it is carefully managed. The subspecies was nearly wiped out by settlers in the late 1800s.

A Cape mountain zebra rolls in a meadow in the De Hoop Nature Reserve in South Africa. The reserve lies on the coast and hosts endangered birds and marine life as well as zebras.

Adult plains zebras surround a foal as they gallop through Masai Mara.

it grows each year. South Africa has recently expanded Mountain Zebra National Park to provide more room for the animals.

The African continent is a tapestry of nations, each with its own identity and goals. Most likely, zebras' numbers will decrease in some nations and grow in others, depending on the actions of the local people. If free herds of wild zebras are to remain in Africa as a whole, however, *many* nations will need to invest their time, money, and determination.

GLOSSARY

arid: not having enough water for many plants to grow

bachelor bands: bands of zebras made up of only stallions

bands: small groups of zebras

camouflage: a color pattern that blends in with the surroundings and acts like a disguise

carnivores: meat eaters

dominant: most powerful

endangered: in danger of dying out

equids: members of the genus *Equus.* Zebras, horses, and assesare all equids.

estrus: a period of time in which a female zebra's body is ready to mate

foals: young zebras

genus: a group of living things that are different but very closely related. Zebras belong to the genus *Equus.*

graze: to feed on new grass and other plants

habitat: the place where an animal or plant is normally found

harems: bands of zebras made up of one stallion, several mares, and their offspring

herbivores: plant eaters

home range: a large area in which zebras live throughout the year

hybrid: the offspring of two animals of different species. A mule is a hybrid whose father is a donkey and whose mother is a horse.

incisor: front biting teeth

interbred: mated with one another

mares: female zebras

migrations: movements of animals from one area to another

nutrients: substances that are needed for the life and growth of plants or animals

nutritious: having value as food

predators: animals that hunt and eat other animals

prey: animals that are hunted by other animals

rank: a zebra's social position compared to other zebras

savanna: a flat, open area with few trees

scavenging: eating the bodies of animals that have already died

stallions: male zebras

species: a group of living things that shares certain characteristics and can mate and produce healthy young

subspecies: groups within a species that share some characteristics that set them apart from the rest of the species

territory: an area of land that a stallion defends against other stallions

wean: to encourage a young animal to eat food other than milk

zoologists: scientists who study animals

SELECTED BIBLIOGRAPHY

Hack, Mace A., and Daniel Rubenstein. "Zebra Zones." *Natural History,* March 1998, 26–33.

Jackman, Brian. *The Marsh Lions.* London: Elm Tree Books, 1982.

MacClintock, Dorcas. *A Natural History of Zebras.* New York: Charles Scribner's Sons, 1976.

Moehlman, Patricia D., ed. *Equids: Zebras, Asses, and Horses: Status Survey and Conservation Action Plan.* Cambridge, UK: IUCN (World Conservation Union), 2002.

Nowak, Ronald M. *Walker's Mammals of the World.* 6th ed. Baltimore: Johns Hopkins University Press, 1999.

Ruxton, Graeme D. "The Possible Benefits of Striped Coat Coloration for Zebra." *Mammal Review* 32, no. 4 (2002): 237–244.

Plains zebras on a misty morning during the rainy season

WEBSITES

Antelope

http://www.sandiegozoo.org/animalbytes/t-antelope.html

This website has photos, fun facts, and more.

Fossil Horse Cybermuseum

http://www.flmnh.ufl.edu/natsci/vertpaleo/fhc/firstCM.htm

This online museum has information on the Equidae family, including an interactive fossil horse gallery, information about fossil digs, and more.

Lions

http://kids.nationalgeographic.com/Animals/CreatureFeature/Lion

This website includes facts, photos, maps, and video.

Mountain Zebra

http://www.kidsplanet.org/factsheets/zebra.html

This species fact sheet has lots of information about the mountain zebra, including information on its size, population, food, behavior, and more.

Zebra

http://animals.nationalgeographic.com/animals/mammals/zebra.html

This National Geographic page has fast facts, a sound bite, and photos.

FURTHER READING

Darling, Kathy. *Lions*. Minneapolis: Lerner Publications Company, 2000.

Grimbly, Shona. *Zebras*. New York: Benchmark Books, 1999.

Lindblad, Lisa. *The Serengeti Migration: Africa's Animals on the Move*. New York: Hyperion Books for Children, 1994.

Markle, Sandra. *Crocodiles*. Minneapolis: Lerner Publications Company, 2004.

———. *Lions*. Minneapolis: Lerner Publications Company, 2005.

———. *Zebras*. Minneapolis: Lerner Publications Company, 2007.

Noble-Goodman, Katherine. *Zebras*. New York: Benchmark, 2006.

Patent, Dorothy Hinshaw. *Horses*. Minneapolis: First Avenue Editions, 1994.

Sayre, April Pulley. *Good Morning, Africa!* Minneapolis: First Avenue Editions, 2003.

INDEX

ABOUT THE AUTHOR

Lynn M. Stone, an author and wildlife photographer, has written more than 400 books for young readers about wildlife and natural history. Stone enjoys fishing and travel and, of course, photographing wildlife. He is a former teacher and lives with his family in Saint Charles, Illinois.

PHOTO ACKNOWLEDGEMENTS

The images in this book are reproduced through the courtesy of: © Andy Rouse/Riser/Getty Images, pp. 2–3; © John R. Kreul/Independent Picture Service, pp. 4, 5, 8, 15, 40 (bottom); © PhotoDisc/Getty Images, pp. 6, 12, 33, 45; © Gerald & Buff Corsi/Visuals Unlimited, p. 7 (top); © Tony Camacho/Photo Researchers, Inc., p. 7 (bottom); © The Natural History Museum/Alamy, p. 9; © AfriPics.com/Alamy, p. 10 (top); © Ariadne Van Zandbergen/Alamy, p. 10 (bottom), 23 (bottom), 32 (top); © Laura Westlund/Independent Picture Service, p. 11; © Gregory G. Dimijian/Photo Researchers, Inc., p. 13 (top); © Art Wolfe/Photo Researchers, Inc., p. 13 (bottom); © Bobby Haas/National Geographic/Getty Images, p. 14; © Anup Shah/naturepl.com, pp. 16, 43; © david tipling/Alamy, pp. 17, 20 (top); © Fritz Polking/Visuals Unlimited, pp. 18 (left), 36 (bottom); © Jim Tampin/Alamy, p. 18 (right); © age fotostock/SuperStock, pp. 19, 23 (top); © Norbert Rosing/National Geographic/Getty Images, p. 20 (bottom); © Charles V. Angelo/Photo Researchers, Inc., p. 21; © Royalty-Free/CORBIS, pp. 22, 26 (bottom), 29, 34; © Kumar Sriskandan/Alamy, p. 24 (top); © David Boag/Alamy, p.24 (bottom); © Nigel J. Dennis/Photo Researchers, Inc., p. 25; © Peter Arnold, Inc./Alamy, p. 26 (top); © Cheryl Ertelt/Visuals Unlimited, p. 27 (left); © simon greetham/Alamy, p. 27 (right); © Mitch Reardon/Photo Researchers, Inc., p. 28; © Wolfgang Kaehler/CORBIS, p. 30 (top); © Images of Africa Photobank/Alamy, p. 30 (bottom), 40 (top); © Joe McDonald/Visuals Unlimited, pp. 31 (top), 36 (top); © Len Rue, Jr./Photo Researchers, Inc., pp. 31 (bottom), 37 (top); © Will Troyer/Visuals Unlimited, p.32 (bottom); © Adam Jones/Visuals Unlimited, p. 35 (top); © Stephen J. Krasemann/Photo Researchers, Inc., p. 35 (bottom); © John Eastcott & Yva Momatiuk/National Geographic/Getty Image, p. 37 (bottom); © Mark Boulton/Photo Researchers, Inc., p. 38; © Peter Jordan/Alamy, p. 39; © Travel Ink/Alamy, p. 41 (top); © Piotr & Irena Kolasa/Alamy, p. 41 (bottom); © Martin Harvey/CORBIS, p. 42

Front Cover © Art Wolfe/Stone/Getty Images
Back Cover © Photodisc/Getty Images